Conte

Tools and Techniques

Hooks are the key component to crochet construction. These come in two classifications: yarn hooks, which are used for all of the projects in this book (and most of the others you'll find elsewhere) and steel hooks that are used solely with crochet thread for lacemaking and filet techniques. Both styles are comprised of different sections: The tip and throat (the hooked end), which are used to make the stitch, the shaft, which determines the size of the hook, and the handle, which is used to hold the hook.

Yarn hooks can be found in aluminum, plastic and acrylic or in natural materials like wood, bamboo and bone. Some have ergonomically shaped handles and cushioned grips that make it easier and more comfortable to work. Start with the old-fashioned aluminum style and as you gain skill and confidence, try experimenting with other styles to see which you like best.

The size of the hook (in combination with the yarn you are using for the project) will determine the size of your stitches. On most hooks, you'll find the size stamped on the handle. In the U.S., hooks are sized by letter of the alphabet, except for size 7 (why, we don't know. It's one of the great mysteries of life). As the letter goes up, so does the size of the hook. Steel hooks are sized by number and reverse the equation. The larger the number, the smaller the hook. The number next to the letter is the equivalent knitting needle size. Generally the smaller hooks are used with thinner yarns and vice versa. The yarn industry has taken some of the confusion out of matching yarn to hook by setting up a standardized system of weights and categories. You can read more about it on page 28.

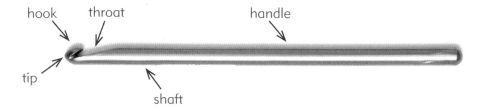

Getting a Grip

The first thing you are going to have to do is learn to hold the hook properly. Easy enough, right? So take your pick from one of these two:

The **knife grip** is the most recommended. With the tip and throat facing you, put your dominant thumb flat on the front of the grip and your index finger flat on the back. Now wrap your remaining fingers around the handle.

Your second choice is the **pencil grip**, which looks a little more elegant, but is not quite as comfortable and is prone to putting strain on your hands. So with the caveat that this grip may cause carpal tunnel, here's how it works. Hold the hook between your dominant thumb and index finger with the remaining fingers folded down, just as you would a pencil.

Hold It Right There

Once you've figured out how to hold the hook you are ready to put it together with your yarn. It all begins with a **slip knot**, the little loop that anchors the yarn to the hook. First, make a loop, placing one end of the yarn centered underneath the loop. (The result, if flattened, will look like a pretzel.) Next, insert the hook under the center strand and pull it up into a loop on the hook (see photo). Pull both yarn ends to tighten the knot on the hook.

Base Camp

We promise we'll get to the fun stuff soon, but for now, you'll have to content yourself with laying the **foundation chain (ch)** for all those stitches to come. This is simply a series of **loops** (called **chain (ch) stitches**) that link together. Crochet is all in the wrists, so relax and let's get started.

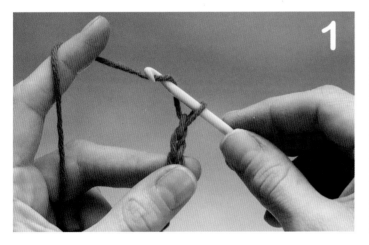

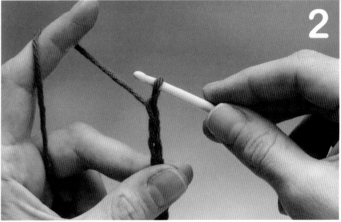

1 Lay the long end of the yarn over the hook from back to front.

2 Catch the yarn under the hook and draw the yarn through the loop.

TIP
Every time you've made four or five stitches, move your thumb and middle finger up and resecure the foundation chain (ch) by holding the last stitch made between these two fingers. Your thumb and middle finger should never be more than 1½"/4cm from the tip of the hook.

Starter Stitches

Now that you've got the foundation chain (ch) down, you're ready to start stitching. Well, almost. First we need to explain a little bit more about what that foundation chain (ch) is, and what it's for.

A foundation chain (ch) has two sides. The side facing as you chain (ch) is call the top. And along the top the stitches form a line of little "V"s, and each "V" has two strands: the strand that's nearest you (the right) is called the front loop, the strand farthest from you (the left) is called the back loop. The new stitches you form will be worked into these loops.

The side opposite the top is called the bottom (no surprise there, right?). On the bottom, the chain (ch) stitches form a single line of bumps. If you look at them closely you'll see that they are actually loops too. They are called—yes you guessed it—the bottom loops. Down the road you may encounter a few projects that call for crocheting into the bottom loops, but for now we'll stick to the top.

Add It Up

When you count crochet stitches (and you'll be doing this a lot) always count from the first stitch after the hook to the last stitch before the slip knot. In other words, the loop that's on the hook is not counted as a chain (ch) stitch, nor is the slip knot. We'll make it a bit clearer with the illustration below:

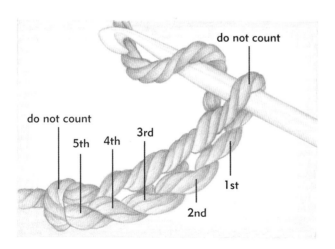

do not count

5th 4th 3rd

do not count

1st

2nd

Over the next several pages we'll be teaching you a few basic stitches, with each stitch getting progressively taller. This is important because which chain (ch) stitch you dip into to make your first crochet stitch will depend on the height of the finished stitch. So since one chain (ch) stitch equals the height of a single crochet (sc) stitch (which we'll cover in a minute), you'll make your first stitch into the second chain (ch) stitch from the hook. For a half-double crochet (hdc) stitch you'll need two chain (ch) stitches to equal the height, so you will dip your hook into the third stitch from the hook. Confused? Don't worry. The pattern directions will always tell you where to begin.

Single Crochet

Now we are going to show you that most basic of crochet stitches, the **single crochet (sc)**.

Start by making a foundation chain (ch) of 11 stitches, holding the **foundation chain (ch)** so that the top is facing you and your thumb and middle finger are holding the third stitch from the hook. Now follow the pictures and instructions below and we'll get you going.

1 Insert the hook under both the front and back loops of the second chain (ch) from the hook. Wrap the yarn over the hook from back to front [this is called a yarn over (yo)] and catch it on the hook. Now draw the hook through the two chain (ch) stitch loops. Like magic, you will now have two loops on the hook

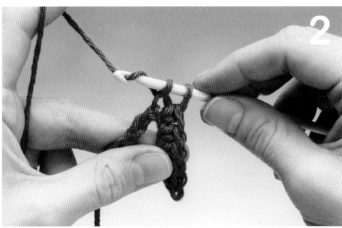

2 Wrap the yarn over the hook from the back to the front [yarn over (yo)], then draw the yarn-over through both loops on the hook.

3 You have now completed one single crochet (sc) stitch. (That wasn't so hard, was it?) Now repeat steps 1 and 2 nine more times, inserting the hook into each chain (ch) stitch across. You will now have ten single crochet (sc) stitches completed across the row.

Chain It Up

Now it's time to move on to the next row. Make one chain (ch) stitch [this is called the turning chain (ch)], then turn the piece from the right to the left. In crochet lingo this is called "chain and turn." For the next row, insert the hook under both the front and back loops of the first stitch (skipping the one turning stitch). Repeat these steps until you have completed 10 rows of single crochet (sc).

TIP
Remember that one chain (ch) stitch equals the height of the single crochet (sc) stitch and that you will always turn the piece from right to left.

The End

When you've completed the number of rows or achieved the length called for in your pattern instructions, you'll need to secure the last stitch so that all your hard work doesn't unravel. This is called fastening off, and it's very easy to do.

1 Start by cutting the yarn about 12" from the last loop on the hook. Bring the remaining yarn over the hook.

2 Draw the tail all the way through the loop on the hook. Pull the tail to tighten and voilá! Your stitches are safe and secure.

Now that you know how to both start a stitch and finish it off, we're going to give you a few easy projects to try. Before you dive in, you should make yourself a gauge swatch, which is a test run of how your pattern, yarn, hook and stitching style all work together. Start by gathering up the exact yarn and needles you intend to use for the project. Chain (ch) enough stitches to create a square at least 4"/10cm wide. Anywhere from 12–20 depending on the size of the hook and the thickness of the yarn you are using should do it. Then work in the specified pattern until the square is a little more than 4"/10cm high.

Put the swatch down on a table or other smooth, hard surface. Use a tape measure or ruler to measure 4"/10cm across the swatch. Count the number of stitches in those 4"/10cm. This will give you the number of stitches.

Now, measure from the bottom to the top of the swatch and count the number of rows in those 4"/10cm. This will give you the number of rows.

Compare these numbers to those in the gauge given for your pattern. If they match, you are ready to get started! If they don't, you'll have to change your hook size and try again. If you were short a few stitches, try using a smaller hook, and if you had too many stitches, try using a larger hook. Try different hook sizes until you get the correct gauge.

Getting Fancy
Half Double, Double and Treble Crochet

You can single crochet (sc) your way through any number of fabulous projects, but let's push the envelope a little, shall we? Now don't get all panicky on us; what we are going to introduce in this chapter takes a little more skill and concentration than the old single crochet (sc), but the stitches are still pretty basic.

Make Mine a Half Double

Remember how we told you crochet stitches kind of build on each other in height? Well we are going to put that theory into practice with a few new stitches. First up is the **half double crochet (hdc)**, for which we'll learn on a foundation chain (ch) of 12 stitches. Got that done? Good. Now let's move on:

1 To begin a half-double crochet (hdc) stitch, yarn over (yo).

2 Insert hook under the top 2 loops of the next stitch and yarn over (yo).

3 Draw yarn-over (yo) through stitch; yarn over (yo) again.

4 Draw yarn-over (yo) through all 3 loops on the hook.

Twice as Nice: Double Crochet

The **double crochet (dc)** stitch adds one more step to those you've completed in the half double crochet (hdc) (which, by the way, is how the half double got its name). Let's start by making a foundation chain (ch) of 13 stitches, then follow the pictures below:

1 To begin a double crochet (dc) stitch, yarn over.

2 Insert hook under the 2 top loops of the next stitch and yarn over (yo) again.

3 Draw the yarn-over (yo) through the stitch—3 loops are on hook; yarn over (yo) again.

4 Draw yarn-over (yo) through first 2 loops; yarn over (yo).

5 Draw yarn-over (yo) through last 2 loops on hook.

We're in Treble

The next stitch we'd like you to meet is the **treble crochet (tr)**. This one builds on the double crochet (dc) stitch you learned earlier (beginning to see a pattern here?). To begin your first practice row make a foundation chain (ch) of 14 stitches, then follow these easy (really!) steps.

1 To begin a treble crochet (tr) stitch, yarn over (yo) twice.

2 Insert hook under the 2 top loops of the next stitch and yarn over (yo) once again.

3 Draw yarn-over through the stitch; yarn over (yo) once again.

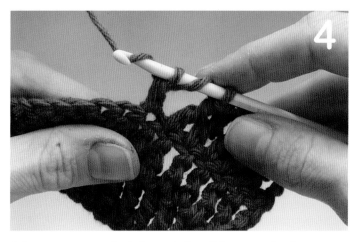

4 Draw yarn-over (yo) through first 2 loops on hook; yarn over (yo) once again.

5 Draw yarn-over (yo) through next 2 loops, yarn over.

6 Draw yarn-over (yo) through last 2 loops on hook.

Slip Shape

Ready for one more? Let us introduce the **slip stitch (sl st)**, a crochet oddity that's more about function than form. You'll use it to anchor chain (ch) stitches, shape pieces, make cording, join stitches when working in the round, secure seams, finish edges and a whole lot more. Every once in a while you'll see it used in pattern stitches, but it's never worked on its own in multiple rows. To try this out, make a foundation chain (ch) of 11 stitches, then follow the simple steps below:

1 Insert the hook under both loops of the second chain from the hook. Yarn over (yo) the hook. Our sample shows working a slip stitch (sl st) into a row of single crochet (sc).

2 Draw through the chain (ch) stitch, then the loop on the hook in one movement. You've made one slip stitch (sl st).

TIP

It's easy to lose track of how many chain (ch) stitches you've made and how many are still left to make. To keep things straight, make yourself a cheat sheet. Write down the number of stitches you have to make on a sheet of paper. Each time you complete ten stitches, make a check mark on the paper. Continue until you reach the number of stitches called for in the pattern—so if you need 60 stitches, you'll have six check marks on your cheat sheet. Get it?

Ups and Downs
Increasing and Decreasing

Sticking to the straight and narrow is just fine and dandy—if you want to crochet nothing more than skinny scarves and belts. (And hey, if you do, we're just fine with it.) But should you decide you want to branch out into something a little more shapely, say a sweater, you'll need to learn to add and subtract stitches, commonly known in the crochet world as increasing and decreasing.

Gain Some—The Increase

Let's start with the increase. There are several ways to add stitches to your row; which method you use depends on where the stitch is being added.

Increasing in the Row

Really this is nothing more than working 2 or more stitches into one stitch. Confused? Don't be. Simply work 2 stitches into the first stitch and 2 stitches into the last stitch. You have now increased 1 stitch at each side of the row

Increasing at the Beginning of a Row

You'll use this method when you need to add a stitch or two at the start of a row.

1 Make the number of chain (ch) stitches you need to increase, then chain (ch) for the height of the stitches you are working in. Here, 3 stitches are going to be increased at the beginning of a single crochet (sc) row, so chain (ch) 3 for the increase and chain (ch) one for the height of the single crochet (sc) stitch—4 chain (ch) stitches in total.

2 Work 1 single crochet (sc) in the 2nd chain (ch) from the hook, then work 1 single crochet (sc) in each of the next 2 chain (ch) stitches—3 single crochet (sc) stitches made. Continue to work across the rest of the row.

Increasing at the End of Row

When you need to add stitches at the end of a row, you do this:

1 To make the first increase stitch, insert the hook under the left vertical strand of the last single crochet (sc) stitch. Yarn over (yo) and draw up a loop. Yarn over (yo) and draw through both loops on the hook to complete the new single crochet (sc) stitch.

2 To make the next and all following increase stitches, insert the hook under the left vertical strand of the last single crochet (sc) stitch made. Yarn over (yo) and draw through both loops on the hook to complete the new single crochet (sc) stitch.

Lose Some—The Decrease

Now, let's move on to the decrease. As with the increase, you can do this several ways, each dependent on where the stitches need to be taken away.

Decreasing in the Row

The idea here is to work each stitch to within the last step to complete it, leaving the last loop (or loops) on the hook. You then yarn over (yo) and draw through all the loops on the hook to combine two (or more) stitches into one. Got it? No? Then let's go through it step by step:

Decreasing 1 Single Crochet

1 Insert the hook into the next stitch and draw up a loop. Insert the hook into the following stitch and draw up a loop.

2 Yarn over (yo) and draw through all three loops on the hook. One single crochet (sc) stitch is decreased.

Decreasing 1 Half Double Crochet

1 Yarn over (yo), insert the hook into the next stitch and draw up a loop. Yarn over (yo), insert the hook into the following stitch, and draw up a loop.

2 Yarn over (yo) and draw through all five loops on the hook. One half double crochet (hdc) stitch is decreased.

Decreasing 1 Double Crochet

1 [Yarn over (yo). Insert the hook into the next stitch and draw up a loop. Yarn over (yo) and draw through two loops on the hook] twice.

2 Draw yarn-over (yo) through all three loops on the hook. One double crochet (dc) stitch has been decreased.

Decreasing 1 Treble Crochet

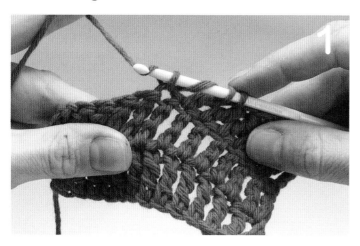 

1 *Yarn over (yo) the hook twice. Insert the hook into the next stitch and draw up a loop. Yarn over (yo) draw through two loops on the hook, then yarn over (yo) again and draw through two loops on the hook*. Repeat from * to * in the following stitch.

2 Yarn over (yo) and draw through all three loops on the hook. One treble crochet (tr) stitch has been decreased.

Decreasing at the Beginning of a Row

If you need to eliminate stitches at the beginning or end of a row, do it like this: Complete the last row before the decrease, then just turn the work (don't chain!). Work one slip stitch (sl st) (remember those?) in each stitch that is to be decreased. Then chain (ch) for the height of the stitch you are working in (one for single, two for half double, etc.) and continue to work across the row.

Decreasing at the End of a Row

If your stitches need to be eliminated at the end of a row, work across the row to the last number of stitches to be decreased and leave them unworked. Chain (ch) and turn to work the next row.

Round and Round
Medallions and More

Up until this point we've been playing it straight, stitching along in nice even rows. Now, let's take crocheting in the round for a spin. To do this you can work in a spiral or joined rounds. Once you master these two techniques you pave the way for a whole new world of crochet possibilities: hats, booties, bags, not to mention the ever-popular granny square. Rounds can shape up into a single item (a hat for instance) or you can connect several smaller ones to create a kind of circular patchwork piece. You can also use them to make fab flowers, medallions and lots of other lovelies.

Make a Ring

No matter what you are making or which method you're using, all rounds start with a ring. Whether that ring is a tightly closed circle (the crown of a hat for example) or an open tube (say a sleeve cuff) depends on the number of chain (ch) stitches you start with. We'll demonstrate with a tight start:

1 To make a practice ring, chain (ch) 6. Insert the hook through both loops of the first chain (ch) stitch made. Yarn over (yo) and draw through the chain (ch) stitch and the loop on the hook in one movement.

2 You have now joined the chain (ch) with a slip stitch (sl st) and formed a ring.

Spiraling

Spirals are worked around and around without interruption, usually in single (sc) or half double (hdc) crochet (this is so there won't be a big difference in height at the beginning and end of the round).

1 Chain (ch) five. Join the chain (ch) with a slip stitch (sl st), forming a ring. Work 10 single crochets (sc) into the ring. Fasten a safety pin in the last stitch made to indicate the end of a round.

2 Work 2 single crochets (sc) in each of the first 9 stitches. Unfasten the safety pin from the last stitch. Work 2 single crochets (sc) in the last stitch. Refasten the safety pin in the last stitch made—you now have 20 stitches. To practice one more round, *work 1 single crochet (sc) in the next stitch, then work 2 single crochets (sc) in the following stitch. Repeat from the * to the end of the round, unfastening, then refastening the safety pin in the last stitch—you now have 30 stitches.

TIP
While you are spiraling it can be tricky to keep track of increases from one round to the next. Use a split- ring marker or small safety pin to mark the end of each round and keep count on a pad of paper as you go.

Simple Flower How-To

You can change yarns and colors within rounds to create some pretty striking pieces that can be used on their own or stitched together to make a larger piece of fabric. Here's how to create a fab flower.

1 To begin this flower, chain (ch) 5. Insert crochet hook into first chain made, as shown above. Then yarn over (yo) the hook, pull up a loop and pull through the loop on the hook to make a ring.

Working Joined Rounds

Joined rounds can be used for any height stitch because the beginning and end of each round is always equal in height. Essentially a series of concentric circles, each round begins with chain (ch) stitches that equal the height of the stitch being used. A slip stitch (sl st) in the first stitch joins the round and completes the circle. It's a little harder to work than a spiral, but since you can see where each round begins and ends, it's also easier to keep track of your increases.

1 Chain (ch) 5. Join the chain (ch) with a slip stitch (sl st), foming a ring. Chain (ch) 3 (equals the height of a double crochet (dc) stitch). Work 12 double crochets (dc) in the ring, then join the round with a slip stitch (sl st) in the top two loops of the first stitch.

2 For the second round, chain (ch) 3. Work 2 double crochet (dc) in each of the 12 stitches. Join the round with a slip stitch (sl st) in the first stitch—you now have 24 stitches. To practice one more round, chain (ch) 3, *work 1 double crochet (dc) in the next stitch, then work 2 double crochet (dc) in the following stitch. Repeat from the * to the end of the round. Join the round with a slip stitch (sl st) in the first stitch—you now have 36 stitches.

2 To make the first round, chain (ch) 3, which counts as the first half double crochet (hdc) and chain (ch) 1; continue to work [1 half double crochet (hdc) and chain (ch) 1] 11 times. You will have 12 half double crochet (hdc) and 12 chain-1 (ch-1) spaces. Join the round by working a slip stitch (sl st) into the 2nd chain (ch) of the beginning chain-3 (ch-3).

3 Shown here is round 3, or the last round. By working [1 single crochet (sc), 2 half double crochet (hdc) and 1 single crochet (sc)] into each chain-1 (ch-1) space from the previous round, you create a ruffled edge.

Great Grannies

For good or bad, the granny square is the motif most people visualize when you mention the word crochet. We'll bet almost everyone you know has an afghan their grandma made them using this nifty variation on the basic crochet round. And like most grannies, she can do a lot of things you never expected of her. Here's how it works:

1

1 With the first color, ch 4. Join ch with a sl st forming a ring. For round 1, ch 3 (counts as 1 dc), working in the ring, work two more dc for the first 3-dc group as shown, then ch 2 for the first corner ch-2 sp.

2

2 To complete the round, [work 3 dc in ring, ch 2] 3 times. This gives you three more 3-dc groups and three more corner ch-2 sps. Join the rnd with a sl st in the top of the beg ch-3 (the first "dc"). Fasten off.

NOTE
As you crochet around, work the dc groups over the tail of the ring or tail from the previous round so you won't have to weave them in later.

3

3 From the RS, join the next color in any corner ch-2 sp with a sl st. (Note: Always alternate the corner you join the color in, so joins are evenly distributed.)

4 For round 2, ch 3 (counts as 1 dc), work 2 dc in the same ch-2 sp (this forms the first half of the first corner), ch 1, [work (3 dc, ch 2, 3 dc) in next ch-2 sp, ch 1] 3 times, at the end work 3 dc in beg ch-2 sp, ch 2 (this forms the second half of the first corner). Join the rnd with a sl st in the top of the beg ch-3. Fasten off. You now have 4 ch-2 corner sps and 4 ch-1 sps (one on each side).

5 Join the next color with a sl st in any corner ch-2 sp. For round 3, ch 3, work 2 dc in same ch-2 sp, ch 1, [work 3 dc in next ch-1 sp, ch 1, work (3 dc, ch 2, 3 dc) in next ch-2 sp, ch 1] 3 times, end work 3 dc in next ch-1 sp, ch 1, work 3 dc in beg ch-2 sp, ch 2. Join rnd with a sl st in top of beg ch-3. Fasten off. You still have 4 ch-2 corner sps, but now you have 8 ch-1 sps (two on each side). For every round that follows, you will increase one ch-1 sp on each side.

Let's Get Together
Joining, Striping and Seaming

While you can crochet away in solitude if you like, but there comes a point where a little meeting of yarns, stitches and pieces must happen.

Tie One On

You've got your crochet full on, cruising along with no worries when suddenly you realize you are about to run out of yarn. What's a girl (or guy) to do? Well dear friends, it is time to learn the joys of joining yarn.

As with knitting you'll want to join your yarn at the end of a row—especially if you're working an openwork or lace stitch where there's no way to weave the ends in invisibly. You may lose some yarn from the previous ball, but you can always use that for seaming fringe or tassels. Here's how it works.

Joining at the End of a Row

To join a new ball of yarn at the side edge, tie it loosely around the old yarn, leaving at least a 6"/15cm tail. Untie the knot later and weave the ends into the seam.

Joining Yarn Midrow

Before joining the new yarn midrow, complete the last stitch that you were working on. Tie the old and new together loosely close to the last stitch; yarn tails should be at least 6"/15cm long. Later, untie the knot and weave in the ends under the stitches.

Stripes: Raising the Bar

You can add some color interest to your projects by working in stripes. How you do this depends on the stitch you are working in, but all the methods are easy enough for even a beginner to master. Let's start with **single crochet (sc)**. Ready to give it a go?

1 Work across the row to within the last stitch. Insert the hook into the last stitch and draw up a loop. Working 6"/15cm from the end of the new color, draw the new color through both loops on the hook to complete the single crochet (sc) stitch.

2 Chain (ch) 1 and turn. Cut the old yarn leaving a 6"/15cm tail. Loosely tie the two tails together, close to the side edge, so stitches don't unravel. Later, untie the knot and weave in the ends.

For **half double crochet (hdc)**, you'll work to within the last stitch, then yarn over (yo), insert the hook into the last stitch and draw up the loop. Then draw the new

color through all three loops on the hook to complete the stitch. Chain (ch) 2 and turn, then join the yarns as in Step 2.

For **double crochet (dc)** you'll work to within the last stitch, then yarn over (yo), insert the hook into the last stitch and draw up the loop. Yarn over (yo) again and draw through first 2 loops. Next, draw the new color through the last two loops on the hook to complete the stitch. Chain (ch) 3 and turn, then join the yarns as in Step 2, above.

For **treble crochet (tr)** you'll work to within the last stitch. Yarn over (yo) the hook twice and draw through two loops on the hook. Yarn over (yo) again and draw through two loops on the hook. Draw the new color through the last two loops on the hook to complete the stitch. Chain (ch) 4 and turn, then join the yarns as in Step 2.

Finishing It Up: Weaving and Blocking

When you join a new ball of yarn or change colors, you'll be left with lots of loose ends. To keep your project from looking scraggly, you will have to weave them all in. It's a tedious but necessary job—we suggest turning on some music or parking yourself in front of the tube to ease the boredom. For threads left hanging at the sides of the work, untie the knot you made when joining the yarn and thread one loose strand into a yarn needle. Insert the needle down through the side edge for about 1½" /4cm, then snip off the excess. Thread the remaining strand through the needle and weave it up in opposite direction. If you changed yarns mid-row, push the knot to the wrong side of the fabric (if it isn't there already). Carefully untie the knot, thread one end of the yarn on a yarn needle and weave the needle horizontally to the right for about three stitches (check on the right side to make sure the weave isn't showing through). Pull

the needle through then take one small backstitch to secure the yarn. Then snip off the excess. Do the same for the remaining loose end, weaving it to left this time.

Once all the pieces for your project are complete, you are ready to start putting the whole thing together. Before you begin you'll need to pin and/or steam you pieces into shape in a process that those in the needlework know call blocking.

Got all that done? Now you can move on to seaming the pieces together. This can be done by sewing, weaving or crocheting them to one another. Your pattern instructions may specify a certain method; if not, choose the one you think will suit the project best. Here are a few of our favorites:

Seams Straightforward

Woven Seam

1 This method gives you an invisible seam with no bulk. Work on a flat surface. With the right sides of both pieces facing you, butt the two edges and secure with safety pins every 2"/5cm. Thread a yarn needle with the tail from the foundation chain. To secure the edges together before weaving, insert the needle from back to front into the corner stitch of the piece without the tail. Making a figure eight with the yarn, insert the needle, from back to front, into the stitch with the tail. Tighten to close up the gap.

2 To begin weaving the seam, insert the needle through the first stitch on the left edge and then through the first stitch on the right edge. Insert the needle through the next stitch on the left edge and then through the next stitch on the right edge. Continue to alternate weaving from edge to edge in this manner, carefully matching stitches (or rows), and drawing the yarn only tight enough the keep the edges together.

Backstitch Seam

1 The backstitch is used when you need a seam that's extra strong and bulk is not an issue. Place the pieces together so the right sides are facing, then pin every 2"/5cm. Thread the tail from the foundation chain (ch) into the yarn needle. Working from back to front, secure the beginning of the seam by taking the needle twice around the bottom edges. Working from back to front again, insert the needle so it exits about ¼"/5mm from the last stitch, as shown.

2 Insert the needle into the same hole as the last stitch, then back up approximately ¼"/5mm in front of the last stitch. Draw the yarn through, then tighten only enough to keep the edges together. Continue to work in this manner, taking care to keep the stitches the same length and straight.

Whipstitch Seam

The whipstitch is used for joining squares for an afghan together, like grannies, as well as other short straight edges. Thread the tail from the foundation chain (ch) in a yarn needle. Place the pieces together so the wrong side sides are facing, edges are even and stitches line up. Insert the needle into the back loop of the piece in front and into the front loop of the adjacent stitch of the piece in back. Continue to work in this manner, drawing the yarn only tight enough the keep the edges together.

Single Crochet Seam

1 Use this method for decorative exterior seams. Working from the ball of yarn, make a slip knot 6"/15cm from the yarn end. Place the slip knot on the hook. To work across top edges, place the pieces together so wrong sides are facing. Working from front to back, insert the crochet hook through both loops of each piece and draw through a loop. Yarn over (yo) and draw through both loops on hook. Continue to work one single crochet (sc) in each pair of adjacent loops across.

2 To work across side edges, place the pieces together so wrong sides are facing. Working through both thicknesses, work single crochet (sc) stitches directly into matching stitches at the side edge, making sure to space them evenly and at the same depth so that all single crochet (sc) stitches are the same size.

Slip Stitch Seam

Use this technique when you want an especially sturdy join, but don't mind the extra bulk. Place the pieces together right sides facing and edges even; pin every 2"/5cm. Working through both thicknesses and from front to back, insert the crochet hook between first two stitches, one stitch in from the edge. Working from the ball of yarn, catch the yarn on the wrong side (about 6"/15cm from the end) and draw through a loop. *Insert the hook between the next two stitches. Draw through a loop, then draw through the loop on the hook. Repeat from the *, keeping an even tension on the yarn so the stitches are even in size and the joining has the same stretchiness as the crocheted fabric.

Finishes & Buttonholes

While there are certainly times when the raw edge of your work will stand on its own, most patterns call for some kind of finish along the edge of your hem, cuff or collar. This can be done with the exact same yarn, a contrasting color or a completely different fiber. (So many choices, so little crocheting time!) Anyway, it's all very easy to do. Read, look and learn as we explain below:

Crocheting Across the Side Edge

When working vertically, crochet stitches directly into the stitches at the side edge. Not only should you make sure to space them evenly, but go into the stitches at the same depth so that all stitches are the same size. If the edging is being added in preparation for seaming (like afghan squares), also take care to work an equal number of edge stitches on all pieces so they'll all match up perfectly.

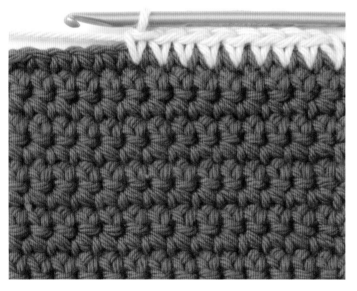

Crocheting Across the Bottom Edge

When working across the bottom edge, work each stitch between two stitches rather than working into the bottom loops of the foundation chain (ch). (Note: Working through the bottom loops will add length, so only work through them when directions tell you to.) If you are using a yarn of a different weight, follow the same technique as described for working across the top edge.

Watch Those Curves

Adding an edging to a curved edge, such as a neckline will take a little more concentration. The basic technique is the same, but the even distribution of stitches becomes even more critical. Here's how to mark for a perfect finish:

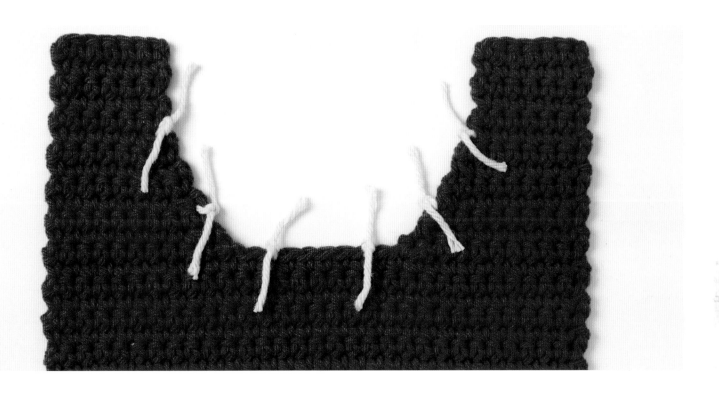

Marking a Curved Edge for Spacing Stitches

Stitches must be distributed evenly so a trim, neckband or collar will not flare out or pull in. Place pins, safety pins, or yarn markers, as shown, every 2"/5cm. If you know the number of stitches to be crocheted, divide this by the number of sections marked to determine how many stitches to work between each pair of markers. If no number is given in the directions, use the marked sections to ensure even spacing around the neck.

TIP

If you are using a thinner yarn to work your edging, you will probably need a smaller hook than the one used for your project. To get things to come out evenly, you'll need to work one stitch in some stitches and two stitches in others. If you are using a thicker yarn, you'll need to use a larger hook and work one stitch in some stitches and skip others to get it all even. You may have to rip out and start over a few times, but don't worry. With practice it'll all work out in the end.

Who's Got the Button

We didn't include any projects with buttonholes in this booklet, but you will come across them at some point. And like every good scout, we want you to be prepared for anything. So here's a quick overview of what it takes to get a buttonhole or two going.

Take Two

The two-row buttonhole is the most common. It can also accommodate just about any size button, which is a nice little perk. Here's how to work it:

1 Work to the placement marker of the buttonhole (single crochet (sc) shown here). Chain (ch) 3 (not too loosely), skip the next 3 stitches, then continue to work to the end of the row or to the next marker.

2 On the next row, work to the chain-3 (ch-3) space. Work 3 stitches in the space, then continue to work to the end of the row or to the next chain-3 (ch-3) space.

Feelin' Loopy

Button loops give a very femme feel to a sweater; they're also sweet on baby things. Here's how to make two basic styles:

One-Step Button Loop

Work to the placement marker of the button loop (single crochet (sc) shown here). Crochet the desired number of chain (ch) stitches (not too loosely), either don't skip any stitches or skip 1 or 2, then continue to work to the end of the row or to the next marker.

Two-Step Button Loop

These very sturdy loops are perfect for fastening just about any size or shape button, and they add a handsome designer detail as well. Make a test swatch following our general directions (below) to familiarize yourself with this technique. To make custom-sized loops, simply adjust the amount of chain (ch) stitches and skipped stitches. After you know how many stitches you must skip, you will then be able to measure and mark for their placement.

1 Work in single crochet (sc) for about 10 stitches. Chain (ch) 4 and turn so the wrong side is facing you. Skip 2 stitches, then work one slip stitch (sl st) in the next stitch.

2 Chain (ch) 1 and turn so the right side is facing you. Work 6 single crochet (sc) in the loop, or as many single crochet (sc) stitches needed to cover the loop. To continue, single crochet (sc) in the next stitch of the edge.

Terms, Abbreviations and Other Useful Stuff

At first glance crochet instructions may seem like they are written is some sort of secret code. They're not. It's just that to save space and make directions a bit clearer, those who write patterns have come up with a few shorthand ways to get the point across. The list below should get you through just about any project. We've also included a handy list of crochet hook sizes and their metric equivalents, as well as a chart listing the different weights of yarn.

standard yarn weight system

Categories of yarn, gauge ranges and recommended needle and hook sizes

Yarn Weight Symbol & Category Names	0 LACE	1 SUPER FINE	2 FINE	3 LIGHT	4 MEDIUM	5 BULKY	6 SUPER BULKY	7 JUMBO
Type of Yarns in Category	Fingering 10-count crochet thread	Sock, Fingering, Baby	Sport, Baby	DK, Light Worsted	Worsted, Afghan, Aran	Chunky, Craft, Rug	Super Bulky, Roving	Jumbo, Roving
Knit Gauge Range* in Stockinette Stitch to 4 inches	33–40** sts	27–32 sts	23–26 sts	21–24 sts	16–20 sts	12–15 sts	7–11 sts	6 sts and fewer
Recommended Needle in Metric Size Range	1.5–2.25 mm	2.25—3.25 mm	3.25—3.75 mm	3.75—4.5 mm	4.5—5.5 mm	5.5—8 mm	8—12.75 mm	12.75 mm and larger
Recommended Needle U.S. Size Range	000–1	1 to 3	3 to 5	5 to 7	7 to 9	9 to 11	11 to 17	17 and larger
Crochet Gauge* Ranges in Single Crochet to 4 inch	32–42 double crochets**	21–32 sts	16–20 sts	12–17 sts	11–14 sts	8–11 sts	6–9 sts	5 sts and fewer
Recommended Hook in Metric Size Range	Steel*** 1.6–1.4 mm	2.25—3.5 mm	3.5—4.5 mm	4.5—5.5 mm	5.5—6.5 mm	6.5—9 mm	9—16 mm	16 mm and larger
Recommended Hook U.S. Size Range	Steel*** 6, 7, 8 Regular hook B–1	B–1 to E–4	E–4 to 7	7 to I–9	I–9 to K–10½	K–10½ to M–13	M–13 to Q	Q and larger

* GUIDELINES ONLY: The above reflect the most commonly used gauges and needle or hook sizes for specific yarn categories.

** Lace weight yarns are usually knitted or crocheted on larger needles and hooks to create lacy, openwork patterns. Accordingly, a gauge range is difficult to determine. Always follow the gauge stated in your pattern.

*** Steel crochet hooks are sized differently from regular hooks—the higher the number, the smaller the hook, which is the reverse of regular hook sizing

skill level

BEGINNER   EASY   INTERMEDIATE   EXPERIENCED

crochet hooks

U.S.	Metric	U.S.	Metric	U.S.	Metric	U.S.	Metric
0	2mm	5	3.75mm	10	6mm	17	12.75mm
1	2.25mm	6	4mm	10½	6.5mm	19	15mm
2	2.75mm	7	4.5mm	11	8mm	35	19mm
3	3.25mm	8	5mm	13	9mm		
4	3.5mm	9	5.5mm	15	10mm		

abbreviations

[ ] or ( )	work directions in brackets or parentheses the number of times indicated	hdc	half double crochet (U.K. htr—half treble crochet)
* or **	repeat directions following * or ** as many times as indicated	hdc2tog	half double crochet 2 sts together
approx	approximately	inc	increase(d)/(ing)
beg	begin(ing)	lp(s)	loop(s)
bet	between	m	meters
bl	back loop	mm	millimeters
BP	back post	MC	main color
BPdc	back post double crochet	oz	ounces
BPsc	back post single crochet	pat(s)	pattern(s)
BPtr	back post treble crochet	pm	place marker
CC	contrasting color	rem	remain(ing)
ch(s)	chain(s)	rep	repeat
ch-	refers to chain or space previously made (i.e., ch-1 space)	rev	reverse
		rev sc	reverse single crochet (U.K. rev dc—reverse double crochet)
ch-sp	chain space previously made		
cl	cluster	rnd(s)	round(s)
cm	centimeters	RS	right side
dc	double crochet (U.K. tr—treble crochet)	sc	single crochet (U.K. dc—double crochet)
dc2tog	double crochet 2 sts together	sc2tog	single crochet 2 sts together
dec	decrease(ing)	sk	skip(ped)
dtr	double treble crochet (U.K. trip tr or trtr—triple treble crochet)	sl	slip
		sl st	slip stitch(es) (U.K. sc—single crochet)
		sp(s)	space(s)
fl	front loop	st(s)	stitch(es)
foll	follow(s)(ing)	t-ch	turning chain
FP	front post	tog	together
FPdc	front post double crochet	tr	treble crochet (U.K. dtr—double treble crochet)
FPsc	front post single crochet		
FPtr	front post treble crochet	trtr	triple treble (U.K. qtr—quadruple treble crochet)
g	grams		
grp(s)	group(s)	WS	wrong side
		yo	yarn over (U.K. yoh—yarn over hook

Fluff Piece

Pompoms

Ahh, the pompom. Plump, plush and ever so perky. Here's how to make a perfect one. You can use pompoms as a decorative trim, at the ends of cords, on hats or hoods, and for children's garments. They are easy to make.

1 With two circular pieces of cardboard the width of the desired pompom, cut a center hole. Then cut a pie-shaped wedge out of the circle.

2 Hold the two circles together and wrap the yarn tightly around the cardboard. Carefully cut around the cardboard.

 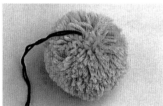

3 Tie a piece of yarn tightly between the two circles. Remove the cardboard and trim the pompom.

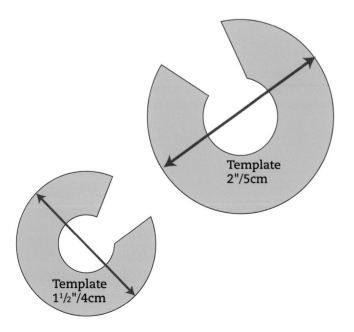

Template 2"/5cm

Template 1 1/2"/4cm

Fringe Benefits

Fringe and tassels work up fast and fabulous. Depending on the type of yarn and where you use it the look can be cowboy cool or showgirl sassy. We're big fans of both.

Simple fringe Cut yarn twice the desired length plus extra for knotting. Fold a cluster of strands (between 2 and 4) in half. On the wrong side, insert the hook from front to back through the piece and over the folded yarn. Pull the fold in the yarn through. Draw the ends through the loop and tighten. Trim the yarn.

Knotted fringe After working a simple fringe (it should be longer to account for extra knotting), take half of the strands from each fringe and knot them with half the strands from the neighboring fringe.

Tassels

Tassel Wrap yarn around cardboard the length of the tassel, leaving a 12"/30cm strand loose at either end. With a yarn needle, knot both sides to the first loop and run the loose strand under the wrapped strands. Pull tightly and tie at the top. Cut the lower edge of the tassel and, holding the tassel about 3/4"/2cm from the top, wind the top strands (one clockwise and one counterclockwise) around the tassel. Thread the two strands and insert them through the top of the tassel.

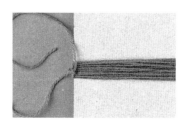 

Easy Projects to Get You Started

Zig Zag Hat

Yarn
5oz/141g or 260yd/240yd of any worsted weight acrylic yarn
• 1 skein each in green (A), pale blue (B), dark blue (C), turquoise (D) and bright blue (E)

Hook
• One size K/10½ (6.5mm) crochet hook *or size to obtain gauge*

LEARN BY VIDEO
www.go-crafty.com
• ch (chain)
• dc (double crochet)
• dc2tog (double crochet 2 sts tog)
• hdc (half double crochet)
• sc (single crochet)
• sc2tog (single crochet 2 sts tog)
• sl st (slip stitch)
• tr2tog (treble crochet 2 sts tog)

MEASUREMENTS
• **Head circumference** 18"/45.5cm
• **Length** 9"/23cm
Note Hat will stretch to fit.

SIZE
One size.

GAUGE
18 sts and 12 rows to 4"/10cm over chevron pat (rnd 3) using size K/10½/6.5mm hook.
Take time to check gauge.

STITCH GLOSSARY
tr2tog *Yo twice, insert hook in next st, yo, pull up a loop, [yo, draw through two loops] twice*, rep from * to * once, yo and draw through all 3 loops on hook.
dc2tog [Yo, insert hook in next st, yo, pull up a loop, yo, draw through two loops] twice, yo and draw through all 3 loops on hook.
sc2tog [Insert hook in next st, yo, pull up a loop] twice, yo and draw through all 3 loops on hook.

NOTES
Hat is worked in the round from lower edge up, then gathered at top. Brim is added afterwards.

HAT
With A, ch 81. Being careful not to twist ch, join with a sl st to first ch.
Rnd 1 (RS) Ch 1, sc in same st as joining and each ch around. Join with sl st to first sc—81 sc.
Rnd 2 Ch 1, sc in same st as joining, sc in next 2 sts, (sc, ch 2, sc) in next st, sc in next 3 sts, *sk next 2 sts, sc in next 3 sts, (sc, ch 2, sc) in next st, sc in next 3 sts; rep from * around to last 2 sts, sk last 2 sts, join with sl st to first sc.
Rnds 3–6 Sl st in next sc, ch 1, sc in same st and next 2 sc, *(sc, ch 2, sc) in next ch-2 sp, sc in next 3 sc, sk 2 sts, sc in next 3 sc; rep from * to last 2 sts, sk last 2 sts, join with sl st to first sc.
Rnds 7–9 With B, sl st in next sc, ch 1, sc in same st and next 2 sc, *(sc, ch 2, sc) in next ch-2 sp, sc in next 3 sc, sk 2 sts, sc in next 3 sc; rep from * to last 2 sts, sk last 2 sts. Join with sl st to first sc.
Rnds 10–12 Rep rnds 7–9 with C.
Rnds 13–15 Rep rnds 7–9 with D.
Rnds 16–18 Rep rnds 7–9 with E.

Rnd 19 With A, sl st in next sc, ch 3 (counts as first dc), hdc in next st, sc in next st, sl st in ch-2 sp, *sc in next st, hdc in next st, dc in next st, tr2tog over next 2 sts, dc in next st, hdc in next st, sc in next st, sl st in ch-2 sp; rep from * to last 5 sts, sc in next st, hdc in next st, dc in next st, tr2tog over last 2 sts, join with sl st to 3rd ch of beg ch-3.
Rnds 20–22 Ch 1, sc in same st as joining and each st around, join with sl st to first sc—72 sc.
Rnd 23 Ch 1, sc in same st as joining and next 5 sts, sc2tog over next 2 sc, *sc in next 6 sts, sc2tog over next 2 sts; rep from * around. Join with sl st to first sc. Fasten off leaving a long tail for gathering.

Brim
Rnd 1 Working along other side of foundation ch, join A with a sl st to any point. *Sc in next st, hdc in next 2 sts, dc2tog over next 2 sts, hdc in next 2 sts, sc in next st, sl st in next st; rep from * around, join with sl st to first sl st.
Rnd 2 Ch 1, sc in same st as joining and each st around, join with sl st to first sc—72 sc.
Fasten off.

FINISHING
Weave tail through rnd 23 of hat. Pull tightly to gather. Make a 1½"/4cm pompom with A and attach to top. ■

Striped Shells Scarf

Yarn

Any worsted weight wool yarn
• 3½oz/100g or 140yd/130m
each in medium blue (A), aqua
blue (B), yellow-green (C), pink
(D) and dark blue (E)

Hook

• Size K/10½ (6.5mm) crochet
hook *or size to obtain gauge*

▶ **LEARN BY VIDEO**
www.go-crafty.com
• ch (chain)
• dc (double crochet)
• sc (single crochet)

MEASUREMENTS

• **Width** 5½"/14cm
• **Length** 67"/170cm (without fringe)

GAUGE

13 sts and 8 rows to 4"/10cm over shell
st pat using size K/10½ (6.5mm) hook.
Take time to check gauge.

NOTE

When changing colors, work the last 2
loops of the last stitch of the row with
the new color.

STITCH GLOSSARY

Shell Stitch Pattern
**(chain a multiple of 6 plus 2—pat
st after the foundation row is a
multiple of 6 sts plus 1)**
Foundation row (RS) Sc in 2nd ch from
hook, *skip next 2 ch, work 5 dc in next
ch (whole shell made), skip next 2 ch,
sc in next ch; rep from * to end. Ch 3
(counts as 1 dc), turn.
Row 1 Work 2 dc in first st (half shell
made), *skip next 2 dc, sc in next dc,

skip next 2 dc, work 5 dc in next sc; rep
from *, end last rep with 3 dc in last sc
(half shell). Ch 1, turn.
Row 2 Sc in first dc, *skip next 2 dc,
work 5 dc in next sc, skip next 2 dc, sc in
next dc; rep from *, end last rep with sc
in top of t-ch of row below. Ch 3, turn.
Rep rows 1 and 2 for shell st pat.

SCARF

With A, ch 218 sts. Work in shell st pat
in the foll stripes, 1 row each A, B, A, C,
A, D, E, C, E, B, E, working ch 1, turn at
end of last row (row 2 of pat).

Last row With E, sc in first sc, *slip
stitch in next 5 dc, sc in next sc; rep
from * to end. Fasten off.

Fringe

Cut strands of each color approx
20"/51cm long. Using 5 strands for
each fringe, attach fringe to each short
end of scarf, matching the stripe pat. ▪

Rose Callahan

Color-Tipped Cowl

Yarn
Any DK weight wool yarn
- 5¼oz/150g or 345yd/320m each in teal (A) and lime green (B)

Hook
- Size 7 (4.5mm) crochet hook *or size to obtain gauge*

Notions
Stitch markers

LEARN BY VIDEO
www.go-crafty.com
- crocheting in the round
- ch (chain)
- dc (double crochet)
- hdc (half double crochet)
- sc (single crochet)

MEASUREMENTS
- **Circumference** 28"/71cm
- **Length** 12"/30.5cm

GAUGE
Six 3-dc groups and 6 rnds to 4"/10cm over pat st using size 7 (4.5mm) hook. *Take time to check gauge.*

COWL

With A, ch 114. Taking care not to twist ch, join with sl st in first ch to form ring.
Rnd 1 Ch 2 (counts as first hdc), hdc in 2nd ch from hook and in each ch around—114 hdc. Join with a sl st in top of beg ch.
Rnd 2 Ch 2, hdc in each st around—114 hdc

Beg Pat Stitch
Rnd 3 Ch 2 (counts as first dc), 2 dc in sp between next 2 hdc, *sk 2 sp between hdc, 3 dc in next sp; rep from * around, join with a sl st in top of beg ch.
Pat rnd Ch 1 (counts as first sc), in next 2 dc, sc in sp between 3-dc grps, ch 2, 2 dc in same sp, *3 dc in next sp between 3-dc grp; rep from * around, join with sl st in top of beg ch.
Rep pat rnd for 16 rnds more, fasten off. Join B with a sl st in same sp between 3-dc grps as join from previous rnd.

Next rnd Ch 2, 2 dc in same sp, *3 dc in next sp between 3-dc grp; rep from * around, join with sl st in top of beg ch. With B, rep pat rnd for 17 rnds more. Rep rnd 2 twice. Fasten off. ■

Jack Deutsch

35

Crocheted Baskets & Vase Cozy

Yarn

Any worsted weight acrylic yarn
• 4oz/115g or 190yd/175m skein each in pale blue (A), lime (B) and aqua blue (C)

Hook

• Size F/5 (3.75mm) crochet hook *or size to obtain gauge*

LEARN BY VIDEO
www.go-crafty.com
• ch (chain)
• crocheting in the round
• sc (single crochet)
• sc2tog (single crochet 2 sts tog)

SIZES

Small, medium, large baskets and needle cozy.

MEASUREMENTS

• **Circumference of baskets at widest point** Approx 11 (13, 14½)"/28 (33, 37)cm
• **Length of baskets** 1¼"/3cm
• **Circumference of vase cozy at widest point** Approx 10½"/26.5cm
• **Length of vase cozy** 6½"/16.5cm

GAUGE

20 sts and 24 rnds to 4"/10cm over sc using size F/5 (3.75mm) crochet hook. *Take time to check gauge.*

NOTES

1 All rounds are worked in a continuous spiral; do not join rounds with a slip stitch.
2 For vase cozy, we covered a Pom Tea glass.

SMALL BASKET

Rnd 1 With A, ch 2, work 6 sc in 2nd ch from hook.
Rnd 2 Work 2 sc in each sc around—12 sc.
Rnd 3 [Sc in next sc, 2 sc in next sc] 6 times—18 sc.
Rnd 4 [Sc in each of next 2 sc, 2 sc in next sc] 6 times—24 sc.
Rnd 5 [Sc in each of next 3 sc, 2 sc in next sc] 6 times—30 sc.
Rnd 6 [Sc in each of next 4 sc, 2 sc in next sc] 6 times—36 sc.
Rnd 7 [Sc in each of next 5 sc, 2 sc in next sc] 6 times—42 sc.
Rnd 8 [Sc in each of next 6 sc, 2 sc in next sc] 6 times—48 sc.
Rnd 9 [Sc in each of next 7 sc, 2 sc in next sc] 6 times—54 sc.
Turning rnd Ch 1, *sc in back loop only of next st; rep from * around, join with slip stitch to ch 1. Work 2 rnds even in sc.
Next rnd Work in sc, dec 4 sts evenly around—50 sc. Work 2 rnds even in sc.
Last rnd Sc in each of next 4 sc, sc2tog around.
Slip st in 1st and 2nd sc of previous rnd. Fasten off.

MEDIUM BASKET

With C, work rnds 1–9 of small basket.
Rnd 10 [Sc in each of next 8 sc, 2 sc in next sc] 6 times—60 sc.

Rnd 11 [Sc in each of next 9 sc, 2 sc in next sc] 6 times—66 sc.
Turning rnd Ch 1, *sc in back loop only of next st; rep from * around, join with slip stitch to ch 1. Work 2 rnds even in sc.
Next rnd Work in sc, dec 4 sts evenly around—50 sc. Work 4 rnds even in sc.
Last rnd Sc in each of next 4 sc, sc2tog around.
Slip st in 1st and 2nd sc of previous rnd. Fasten off.

LARGE BASKET

With B, work rnds 1–11 of small basket.
Rnd 12 [Sc in each of next 10 sc, 2 sc in next sc] 6 times—72 sc.
Turning rnd Ch 1, *sc in back loop only of next st; rep from * around, join with slip stitch to ch 1.
Work 2 rnds even in sc.
Next rnd Work in sc, dec 4 sts evenly around—68 sc.
Work 4 rnds even in sc.
Last rnd Sc in each of next 4 sc, sc2tog around.
Slip st in 1st and 2nd sc of previous rnd. Fasten off.

VASE COZY

With C, work rnds 1–8 of small basket.
Rnd 9 [Sc in each of next 11 sc, 2 sc in next sc] 4 times—52 sc.
Rnd 10 (turning round) Ch 1, *sc in back loop only of next st; rep from * around, join with slip stitch to ch 1.
Cont to work in rnds of sc in stripes as foll: 12 rnds C, 12 rnds B, 12 rnds A.
Slip stitch in 1st and 2nd st.
Fasten off. ▪

Crocheted Flowers

Yarn

Any worsted weight cotton yarn
- Small amounts in peach (A), light peach (B), deep coral (C) and green (D)
- Small amount of lightweight scrap yarn in pale gray (E) for center of flower with leaves

Hook
- Size F/5 (3.5mm) crochet hook *or size to obtain gauge*

Notions
- One pin back for each flower

LEARN BY VIDEO
www.go-crafty.com
- ch (chain)
- crocheting in the round
- dc (double crochet)
- hdc (half double crochet)
- sc (single crochet)
- sl st (slip stitch)

MEASUREMENTS/GAUGE

For Single-Color Rosette
- **Diameter** 2¾"/7cm

For 3-Color Flower
- **Diameter** 3"/7.5cm

For Flower With Leaves
- **Diameter (without leaves)** 2"/5cm
- **Length of leaf** Approx 1½"/4cm
Take time to check gauge.

NOTE
Use colors as desired.

SINGLE-COLOR ROSETTE
Leaving long tail, chain 35.
Row 1 Dc in 5th ch from hook, *ch 1, skip 1 ch, [dc, ch 1, dc] in next ch—V-st made; rep from * to end, turn—16 V-sts made.
Row 2 Ch 3 (counts as dc), 5 dc in first ch-1 space, *sc in next ch-1 space, 6 dc in next ch-1 space—1 shell st made; rep from * 14 times more—16 shells. Fasten off leaving long tail for sewing.

FINISHING
Coil strip to form rosette. Use long tail to sew tog. Sew pin to back.

3-COLOR FLOWER
With desired color for center of flower, ch 5, join with sl st in first ch to form ring.
Rnd 1 Work 8 sc in ring.
Rnd 2 Ch 3 (counts as 1 dc), *2 dc in next sc; rep from * 6 times more, end 1 dc in next sc, with 2nd color join with sl st in top of ch-3. Do not cut first color.
Rnd 3 With 2nd color, ch 1 *sc in next dc, (hdc, 3 dc, hdc) in next dc; rep from * 7 times more—8 petals. With first color, join with sl st to beg ch 1. Cut 2nd color.
Rnd 4 With first color, and working from behind, ch 2, insert hook from back to front to back around the beg ch-3 from rnd 2 and work 1 sc, ch 5, *skip next dc, work 1 dc around post of next dc in rnd 2 as before, ch 3; rep from * 7 times more. With 3rd color join with sl st in 2nd ch of beg ch 5.
Rnd 5 Ch 1, *(sc, hdc, 3 dc, hdc, sc) in next ch-3 space; rep from * 7 times more, with first color join with sl st in top of ch-3. Cut 3rd color.
Rnds 6 and 7 Rep rnds 4 and 5 with first color, or desired color. Fasten off.

FINISHING
Sew pin to back.

FLOWER WITH LEAVES
Center of Flower
With E, make a slip knot so that pulling the tail (and not the working yarn) tightens the loop.
Rnd 1 Sc 1, ch 2, dc 11 in slip knot. Pull tail to tighten loop. With desired color, join with sl st in top of beg ch-2. Cut first color.

Petals
Rnd 1 *Ch 3, skip next st, sl st in next st; rep from * 5 times more, end ch 1.
Rnd 2 *(Sc, hdc, 3 dc, hdc, sc) in next ch-3 space; rep from * 5 times more, join with sl st to first sc. Fasten off.

Leaves
With D, attach yarn to back of any petal, *insert hook from back to front to back around sl st in rnd 1 and work sc, ch 13, sl st 1 in 2nd ch from hook, [work 3 dc next ch] 9 times, [sc in next ch] twice, ch 2; rep from * until 6 leaves are complete, join with sl st to first st. Fasten off.

FINISHING
Sew pin to back. ■

Rose Callahan

Simple Hat

Yarn
- 3½oz/100g or 230yd/250m of any DK weight wool yarn

Hook
- Size H/8 (5mm) crochet hook *or size to obtain gauge*

LEARN BY VIDEO
www.go-crafty.com
- crocheting in the round
- dc (double crochet)
- sc (single crochet)
- sl st (slip stitch)

MEASUREMENTS
- **Brim circumference** 20"/51cm
- **Length** 8"/20.5cm

GAUGE
16 dc and 9 rnds to 4"/10cm over dc pat st using size H/8 (5 mm) crochet hook. *Take time to check gauge.*

HAT
Ch 4, join with a sl st in first ch to form ring.

Rnd 1 Ch 1, work 8 sc in ring, join with sl st to first sc.

Rnd 2 Ch 3, work 2 dc in each sc around, join to top of ch-3.

Rnd 3 Ch 3 (does not count as 1 dc), *1 dc in first dc, 2 dc in next dc; rep from * around—24 dc (not counting the ch-3). Join to top of ch 3 on this and all foll rnds.

Rnd 4 Ch 3, *1 dc in each of next 2 dc, 2 dc in next dc; rep from * around—32 dc, join.

Rnd 5 Ch 3, *1 dc in each of next 3 dc, 2 dc in next dc; rep from * around—40 dc, join.

Rnd 6 Ch 3, *1 dc in each of next 4 dc, 2 dc in next dc; rep from * around—48 dc, join.

Rnd 7 Ch 3, *1 dc in each of next 5 dc, 2 dc in next dc; rep from * around—56 dc, join.

Rnd 8 Ch 3, *1 dc in each of next 6 dc, 2 dc in next dc; rep from * around—64 dc, join.

Rnd 9 Ch 3, *1 dc in each of next 7 dc, 2 dc in next dc; rep from * around—72 dc, join.

Rnd 10 Ch 3, *1 dc in each of next 8 dc, 2 dc in next dc; rep from * around—80 dc, join.

Next 8 rnds Ch 3, work 1 dc in each dc around, join. Piece measures 7¾"/19.5cm from top of crown.

BRIM
Turn cap to WS and work as foll:

Turning rnd 1 Ch 3, working in back loops only, work 1 dc in each st around.

Rnds 2 and 3 Work even in dc.

Rnd 4 Ch 1, sl st loosely in each st around. Fasten off, tacking the folded brim in place with tail. Tack in place once at opposite side. ■

Crocheted Blanket

Yarn

Any DK weight cotton yarn
- 21oz/600g or 1290yd/1180m
  in yellow (A)
- 7oz/200g or 430yd/395m
  each in grey (B), black (C)
  and white (D)

Hook
- Size 7 (4.5mm) crochet hook
  or size to obtain gauge

Notions
- Locking stitch markers

LEARN BY VIDEO
www.go-crafty.com
- hdc (half double crochet)
- sc (single crochet)
- sl st (slip stitch)
- tr (treble crochet)

MEASUREMENTS
Approx 42 x 66"/106.5 x 167.5cm

GAUGE
14 sts and 12 rows to 4"/10cm over ridge pat using size 7 (4.5mm) crochet hook. *Take time to check gauge.*

STITCH GLOSSARY
Foundation half double crochet (Fhdc)
Ch 3, yo, insert hook in 3rd ch from hook, yo and draw up a lp, yo and draw through 1 lp (1 ch made), yo and draw through all lps on hook, *yo, insert hook under ch of previous st, draw up a lp, yo and draw through 1 lp (1 ch made), yo and draw through all lps on hook; rep from * for desired number of foundation half double crochet.

Spike single crochet (Ssc) Insert hook into work over last 2 rnds just worked, yo and pull up loop to the height of the two rnds, yo and pull through both loops on hook.

Ridge Pattern
Row 1 (RS) Working into front loop only, work 1 hdc in each sl st. Ch 1, turn.
Row 2 Working through frontmost loop (the loop below the top V), work 1 sl st in each st.
Ch 2, turn.
Rep rows 1 and 2 for ridge pat.

BLANKET
With A, Fhdc 144 sts. Ch 1, turn.
Next row (WS) Working sl st in each hdc. Ch 2, turn.
Work in ridge pat in stripes as foll:
10 rows A, 6 rows B, 6 rows C, 6 rows D, 6 rows B, 18 rows A, 6 rows C, 12 rows A, 6 rows D, 12 rows A, 12 rows B, 12 rows A, 6 rows D, 12 rows A, 6 rows C, 18 rows A, 6 rows B, 6 rows D, 6 rows C, 6 rows B, 12 rows A. Do not fasten off, pm in last st.

Edging
Rnd 1 Ch 1, working down side of blanket, work sc in the side of each hdc and sl st row to end, work 3 sc in corner, sc along foundation ch edge, work 3 sc in corner, sc in the side of each hdc and sl st row to end, 3 sc in corner, sc along top edge, 3 sc in marked st (leave marker in place), join with sl st to beg ch-1.
Rnd 2 Ch 1, sc in each sc, working 2 sc in the center sc at each corner, join with sl st to beg ch-1. Fasten off.
Rnd 3 Join B in marked corner space, work Ssc in joining, (ch 1, Ssc, ch 1, Ssc) in same sp, *ch 1, sk 1 st, Ssc; rep from * around, working [ch 1, Ssc] 3 times in each corner, and join with ch-1, sl st in beg ch-1. Fasten off.

MATCHING TIE
With C, ch 153.
Row 1 Sc in 2nd ch from hook and in each ch to end, changing to B on last st—152 sts. Ch 1, turn.
Row 2 Work sc in each st, changing to D on last st. Ch 1, turn.
Row 3 Work sc in each st, changing to A on last st. Ch 4, turn.
Row 4 Work tr in each st, changing to D on last st. Ch 1, turn.
Row 5 Work sc in each st, changing to B on last st. Ch 1, turn.
Row 6 Work sc in each st, changing to C on last st. Ch 1, turn.
Row 7 Work sc in each st. Fasten off. ■

Shell Wristers

Yarn
- 5⅓oz/150g or 350yd/320m of any sport weight self striping wool blend yarn in pinks and greens

Hook
- Size F/5 (3.75mm) hook
- *or size to obtain gauge*

LEARN BY VIDEO
www.go-crafty.com
- ch (chain)
- dc (double crochet)
- sc (single crochet)
- sl st (slip stitch)

MEASUREMENTS
- **Circumference** 7"/17.5cm
- **Length (including edging)** 8½"/21.5cm

GAUGE
3 st reps (sc and 5-dc shell = 1 rep) and 11 rows to 4"/10cm over shell st using size F/5 (3.75mm) hook.
Take time to check gauge.

STITCH GLOSSARY
Shell Stitch (chain a multiple of 6 sts plus 2)
Row 1 Sc in 2nd ch from hook, *skip 2 ch, 5 dc in next ch (shell st), skip 2 ch, sc in next ch; rep from * to end. Ch 3, turn.
Row 2 Work 2 dc in first sc, skip 2 dc, sc in next dc (center of 5-dc shell from previous row), *5 dc in next sc, skip 2 dc, sc in next dc; rep from *, end 3 dc in last sc. Ch 1, turn.
Row 3 Work sc in first dc, *5 dc in next sc, skip 2 dc, sc in next dc (center of 5-dc shell from previous row); rep from

* to end, working last sc in top of t-ch. Ch 3, turn.
Rep rows 2 and 3 for shell st.

LEFT WRISTLET
Ch 38. Work rows 1–3 of shell st, then rep rows 2 and 3 eight times. Do not fasten off.

FINISHING
Turn work and fold foundation up to last row just worked. Join foundation row to last row with sl st, working in shell pat row 2 along working row, as foll:
Joining row (RS) Sl st into sc on foundation row, 2 dc in 1st sc, skip 2 dc, sc in next dc, sl st in base of 5-dc shell on foundation ch, 5 dc in next sc, skip 2 dc, sc in next dc, leave corresponding sc and 5-dc shell on foundation ch unworked (thumb opening made), [3 dc in next sc, sl st in base of corresponding sc on foundation ch, 2 dc in same sc, skip 2 dc, sc in next dc, sl st in base of 5-dc shell on foundation ch] 4 times, 3 dc in next sc, sl st in base of sc on foundation ch.
Fasten off.

Edging
With RS facing, join yarn and work sc in one corner at top of wrister. Working across top opening, alternate 5-dc shell and sc evenly spaced so that there are 6 shells, join rnd with sl st in 1st sc.
Fasten off.

RIGHT WRISTLET
Work as for left wristlet to joining row.
Joining row (RS) Sl st into sc on foundation row, 2 dc in first sc, [skip 2 dc, sc in next dc, sl st in base of 5-dc shell on foundation ch, 3 dc in next sc, sl st in base of corresponding sc on founda-

tion ch, 2 dc in same sc] 4 times, skip 2 dc, sc in next dc, leave corresponding sc and 5-dc shell on foundation ch unworked (thumb opening made), 5 dc in next sc, skip 2 dc, sc in next dc, sl st in base of 5-dc shell on foundation ch, 3 dc in next sc, sl st in base of sc on foundation ch.
Fasten off.
Work edging as for left wristlet. ■

Crocheted Poufs

Yarn

Any super bulky weight
T-shirt yarn
• 18oz/510g or 285yd/260m in
light green for small pouf
• 26oz/740g or 430yd/985m in
bright blue for medium blue
• 35oz/995g or 570yd/520m in
yellow for large pouf

Hook

• Size P/15 (10mm) crochet
hook *or size to obtain gauge*

Notions

• Round pillow form with a
diameter of 14 (16, 18)"/35
(45, 56)cm

LEARN BY VIDEO
www.go-crafty.com
• adjustable ring
• crocheting in the round
• dc (double crochet)
• sl st (slip stitch)

SIZES
Sized for Small, Medium, Large.

MEASUREMENTS
Small Pouf
• **Diameter** 14"/35cm,
• **Height** 6"/15cm

Medium Pouf
• **Diameter** 18"/45cm
• **Height** 7½"/19cm

Large Pouf
• **Diameter** 22"/56cm
• **Height** 8¼"/21cm

GAUGE
8 sts and 4 rnds to 4"/10cm over dc pat
using size P/15 (10mm) crochet hook.
Take time to check gauge.

SPECIAL TECHNIQUES
Adjustable Ring

1 Hold the yarn end with your left
thumb and index finger, wrap the yarn
from the ball down around the back
of your hand and up across the palm
of your left hand.

2 Insert the hook through the yarn
loop from the front and yarn over the
hook.

3 Draw the yarn-over through the loop
to form the ring and work chain 2.

4 Work a single crochet by inserting
hook into the center of ring to draw up
a loop, complete the sc. Continue to
work 11 sc in this way around the ring.

5 Join with slip stitch to top of the beg
ch-2. Pull the short end of the yarn to
close the circle.

Decrease 1 Double Crochet
Yo, insert hook in next st, yo and draw
up a lp, yo and draw through 2 lps on
hook, yo, insert hook in next st, yo and
draw up a lp, yo and draw through 2 lps
on hook, yo and draw through all 3 lps
on hook—1 dc dec'd.

NOTES

1 Ch 2 at beg of rnd counts as first dc.
Always join every rnd with sl st in the
top of beg ch-2.

2 After the last increase row, lay the
piece on the pillow form to check
if the diameter is correct. If it is too
small, continue increasing sts in the
same sequence every row; if it is too
large, take out a row. Before start-
ing the increases, rounds are worked
even to form the height of the pillow.

Adjust the number of these even rows
if necessary.

SMALL POUF
Top Piece
With desired color, make an adjustable
ring and work 11 sc in ring as described
above.

Rnd 2 Ch 2 (counts as first dc), work
1 dc in same place as joining, working
through back lp only, work 2 dc in each
of next 11 sc, join with sl st to top of
beg ch-2—24 dc.

Rnd 3 Ch 2, working through back lp
only, [2 dc in next dc, dc in next dc] 11
times, 2 dc in last dc, join with sl st to
top of beg ch-2—36 dc.

Rnd 4 Ch 2, working through back lp
only, [2 dc in next dc, dc in each of next
2 dc] 11 times, 2 dc in next dc, dc in
last dc, join with sl st to top of beg ch-
2—48 dc.

Rnd 5 Ch 2, working through back lp
only, [2 dc in next dc, dc in each of next
3 dc] 11 times, 2 dc in next dc, dc in
each of last 2 dc, join with sl st to top of
beg ch-2—60 dc.

Rnd 6 Ch 2, working through back lp
only, [2 dc in next dc, dc in each of next
4 dc] 11 times, 2 dc in next dc, dc in
each of last 3 dc, join with sl st to top of
beg ch-2—72 dc.

Rnd 7 Ch 2, working through back lp
only, [2 dc in next dc, dc in each of next
5 dc] 11 times, 2 dc in next dc, dc in
each of last 4 dc, join with sl st to top of
beg ch-2—84 dc.

Next 2 rnds Ch 2, work dc in each dc,
join with sl st to top of beg ch-2—84 dc.

Dec rnd 1 Ch 2, dc in each of next 4
dc, [dec 1 dc, dc in each of next 5 dc]
11 times, dec 1 dc—72 dc.

Dec rnd 2 Ch 2, dc in each of next 3
dc, [dec 1 dc, dc in each of next 4 dc]
11 times, dec 1 dc—60 dc.

Crocheted Poufs

Dec rnd 3 Ch 2, dc in each of next 2 dc, [dec 1 dc, dc in each of next 3 dc] 11 times, dec 1 dc—48 dc.
Dec rnd 4 Ch 2, dc in next dc, [dec 1 dc, dc in each of next 2 dc] 11 times, dec 1 dc—36 dc.
Fasten off.

Under Piece
Work same as Top Piece through rnd 4—48 dc. Fasten off.

FINISHING
Insert pillow form into Top Piece. Lay under piece in place so that the joining of rnds on both pieces line up and sew pieces together.

MEDIUM POUF
Top Piece
Work rnds 1–7 same as Small Pouf—84 dc.
Rnd 8 Ch 2, working through back lp only, [2 dc in next dc, dc in each of next 6 dc] 11 times, 2 dc in next dc, dc in

each of last 5 dc, join with sl st to top of beg ch-2—96 dc.
Rnd 9 Ch 2, working through back lp only, [2 dc in next dc, dc in each of next 7 dc] 11 times, 2 dc in next dc, dc in each of last 6 dc, join with sl st to top of beg ch-2—108 dc.
Dec rnd 1 Ch 2, dc in each of next 3 dc, [dec 1 dc, dc in each of next 4 dc] 17 times, dec 1 dc—90 dc.
Dec rnd 2 Ch 2, dc in each of next 3 dc, [dec 1 dc, dc in each of next 4 dc] 14 times, dec 1 dc—75 dc.
Dec rnd 3 Ch 2, dc in each of next 2 dc, [dec 1 dc, dc in each of next 3 dc] 14 times, dec 1 dc—60 dc.
Fasten off.

Under Piece
Work same as top piece through rnd 7—84 dc. Fasten off.

FINISHING
Insert pillow form into Top Piece. Lay Under Piece in place so that the joining of rnds on both pieces line up and sew pieces together.

LARGE POUF
Top Piece
Work rnds 1–9 same as Medium Pouf—108 dc.
Rnd 10 Ch 2, working through back lp only, [2 dc in next dc, dc in each of next 8 dc] 11 times, 2 dc in next dc, dc in each of last 7 dc, join with sl st to top of beg ch-2—120 dc.
Rnd 11 Ch 2, working through back lp only, [2 dc in next dc, dc in each of next 9 dc] 11 times, 2 dc in next dc, dc in each of last 8 dc, join with sl st to top of beg ch-2—132 dc.
Rnd 12 Ch 2, working through back lp only, [2 dc in next dc, dc in each of next 10 dc] 11 times, 2 dc in next dc, dc in

each of last 9 dc, join with sl st to top of beg ch-2—144 dc.
Next 4 rnds Ch 2, work dc in each dc, join with sl st to top of beg ch-2—144 dc.
Dec rnd 1 Ch 2, dc in each of next 3 dc, [dec 1 dc, dc in each of next 4 dc] 23 times, dec 1 dc—120 dc.
Dec rnd 2 Ch 2, dc in each of next 3 dc, [dec 1 dc, dc in each of next 4 dc] 19 times, dec 1 dc—100 dc.
Dec rnd 3 Ch 2, dc in each of next 3 dc, [dec 1 dc, dc in each of next 4 dc] 15 times, dec 1 dc, dc in next 4 dc—84 dc.
Dec rnd 4 Ch 2, dc in each of next 3 dc, [dec 1 dc, dc in each of next 4 dc] 13 times, dec 1 dc—70 dc.
Fasten off.

Under Piece
Work same as Top Piece through rnd 9—108 dc. Fasten off.

FINISHING
Insert pillow form into Top Piece. Lay Under Piece in place so that the joining of rnds on both pieces line up and sew pieces together. ■

Baby Blocks Blanket

Yarn
3½oz/100g, 220yd/200m of any worsted weight cotton/acrylic blend in light blue (A) and ecru (B) 1¾oz/50g, 110yd/100m in pink (C), purple (D), red (E), orange (F), lime green (G), sage green (H), natural (I), and dark blue (J)

Needles
Size E/4 (3.5mm) crochet hook
or size to obtain gauge

▶ LEARN BY VIDEO
www.go-crafty.com
- ch (chain)
- changing colors
- crocheting in the round
- dc (double crochet)
- sc (single crochet)
- sl st (slip stitch)

MEASUREMENTS
Approx 33 x 33"/83.5 x 83.5cm

GAUGE
1 granny square to 4½"/11.5cm using size E/4 (3.5mm) crochet hook.
Take time to check gauge.

NOTES
1 Colors are used randomly and can be placed as desired OR use the placement diagram that shows the color sequence of each square as shown in the photo. Note that the center square is a solid color, lime green (G). All the other squares change color at the end of every round.

2 When changing colors for each round, dc over yarn tails to hide and then cut. This eliminates weaving in all the tails.

GRANNY SQUARE
Make 49 squares.
Follow the placement diagram for the color sequence of each square or use colors as desired.
Ch 4, join with sl st in first ch to form ring.
Rnd 1 Ch 5, [work 3 dc in ring, ch 2] 3 times, work 2 dc in ring, sl st in 3rd ch of beg ch 5. Fasten off.
Rnd 2 Join new color with sl st into ch-2 sp, ch 5, 3 dc in same sp, *ch 1, (3 dc, ch 2, 3 dc) in next sp; rep from * twice more, ch 1, 2 dc in same sp as beg ch-5, sl st in 3rd ch of ch-5. Fasten off.

Rnd 3 Join new color with sl st into ch-2 sp, ch 5, 3 dc in same sp, *ch 1, 3 dc in next sp, ch 1, (3 dc, ch 2, 3 dc) in next sp; rep from * twice more, ch 1, 3 dc in next sp, ch 1, 2 dc in same sp as beg ch-5, sl st in 3rd ch of ch-5. Fasten off.
Rnd 4 Join new color with sl st into ch-2 sp, ch 5, 3 dc in same sp, *[ch 1, 3 dc in next sp] twice, ch 1, (3 dc, ch 2, 3 dc) in next sp; rep from * twice more, (ch 1, 3 dc in next sp) twice, ch 1, 2 dc in same sp as beg ch-5, sl st in 3rd ch of ch-5. Fasten off.

Baby Blocks Blanket

FINISHING
Block squares to measurement.

Joining Squares
Arrange squares with right sides facing following the placement diagram. With B, single crochet squares together using back loop only of each square. Single crochet all horizontal rows, then vertical rows. Fasten off at the end of each row, except the last seam.

Note Use a sl st when crossing over a previous sc seam.

Edging
Rnd 1 After seaming the last row, cont with B and work 1 sc in each dc and ch-1 sp, and sl st over seams around border of entire blanket. At each corner, work 3 sc in ch-2 sp. End with sl st in first sc of rnd.

Rnd 2 Join A with sl st, ch 1, sc in same st, sc in each sc around entire blanket, 3 sc in each corner st, end with sl st in beg ch-1.

Rnd 3 Ch 2, work hdc in each sc around, working 3 hdc in each corner st, end with sl st in 2nd chain of beg ch-2.

Rnd 4 Ch 1, work sc in each hdc around, working 3 sc in each corner st. End with sl st in beg ch-1.

PLACEMENT DIAGRAM

F, A, G, D	H, B, I, C	J, C, D, G	E, B, D, F	D, H, C, A	J, I, E, D	B, F, A, G
C, A, F, B	D, A, C, I	G, E, A, H	J, F, G, I	E, I, D, C	G, E, C, B	C, D, H, E
I, J, F, E	H, C, A, J	I, H, J, F	C, G, F, D	D, A, I, H	B, J, A, I	F, A, G, C
C, B, D, H	E, B, H, I	F, D, E, J	G	G, I, D, A	J, G, E, B	A, J, C, D
I, B, G, J	A, G, J, H	J, B, A, C	H, C, B, E	F, H, A, B	E, A, B, J	D, A, B, F
A, I, G, E	G, C, A, F	E, C, I, A	F, E, D, I	G, J, F, C	F, B, E, A	I, F, B, H
C, J, G, A	F, E, D, G	G, F, I, J	I, E, H, D	C, I, G, F	I, C, D, B	G, D, A, E

COLOR KEY
A Light blue
B Ecru
C Pink
D Purple
E Red
F Orange
G Lime
H Sage
I Natural
J Dark blue

Crocheted Shawl

Yarn
Any super bulky weight acrylic yarn
- 15oz/430g or 375yd/345m in cream (A)
- 5oz/145g or 125yd/115m each in orange (B) and light grey (C)

Hook
- One size P/Q (15 mm) crochet hook *or size to obtain gauge*

LEARN BY VIDEO
www.go-crafty.com
- ch (chain)
- dc (double crochet)
- dc2tog (double crochet 2 sts tog)
- hdc (half double crochet)
- sc (single crochet)
- sl st (slip stitch)

MEASUREMENTS
- **Width** 64"/162.5cm
- **Depth** 32"/81cm

GAUGE
13 sts = 6"/15 cm and 11 rows = 8"/20.5 cm over dc/sl st pat st using size P/Q (15 mm) crochet hook.
Take time to check your gauge.

STITCH GLOSSARY
Dc2tog [Yo hook and draw up a loop in next st, yo through 2 loops on hook] twice, yo and through all 3 loops—1 st dec'd.

NOTE
The dc/sl st pat st is worked using A (or C) for the dc rows and B for all the sl st rows. Work the sl st rows loosely and drop yarn just worked at the end of the row to be picked up and worked from that side as described.

SHAWL
Beg at outside edge with A, ch 152.

Row 1 (RS) With A, work 1 dc in 3rd ch from hook, [dc2tog] twice, 1 dc in each of next 67 ch, dc2tog, skip 2 ch, dc-2tog, work 1 dc in each of next 67 ch, [dc2tog] twice, 1 dc in last ch, drop A.

Row 2 (WS) With B, ch 1, then working into front loops only, working loosely, work 1 sl st in each st to end, drop B.

Row 3 (WS) Return to the WS and with dropped A, ch 2 (does not count as 1 dc on this or any row), working into both loops, work 1 dc, [dc2tog] twice, then work dc to 3 dc before the center dc (or 63 dc), dc2tog, and skip the center 2 sts, then dc2tog, work 63 dc, [dc2tog] twice, work 1 dc, drop A and turn.

Row 4 (RS) From beg of the RS row and with B, ch 1, work 1 sl st in back loop only of each st to end, drop B.

Row 5 (WS) Join C, ch 2, working into front loops only, work 1 dc, [dc2tog] twice, work 59 dc (or to 3 sts before the center), dc2tog, skip center 2 sts, dc-2tog, work 59 dc, [dc2tog] twice, work 1 dc, cut C.

Row 6 (WS) With dropped B, ch 1, sl st in front loop of each st, drop B

Row 7 (RS) With A, ch 2, working in both loops, work 1 dc, [dc2tog] twice, work 55 dc (or 3 sts before the center), dc2tog, skip center 2 sts, dc2tog, work 55 dc, [dc2tog] twice, work 1 dc, drop A.

Row 8 (RS) With B, ch 1, sl st through back loops only. Drop B.

Row 9 (WS) With A, ch 2, working into front loops only, work 1 dc, [dc2tog] twice, work 51 dc (or 3 sts before the center), dc2tog, skip center 2 sts, dc-2tog, work 51 dc, (dc2tog) twice, work 1 dc, cut A.

Row 10 (WS) With dropped B, rep row 2.

Row 11 (WS) With A, rep row 3 only with 47 (not 63) dc.

Row 12 (RS) With B, rep row 4.

Row 13 (WS) With C, rep row 5 only with 43 (not 59) dc.

Row 14 (WS) With B, rep row 6.

Row 15 (RS) With A, rep row 7 only with 39 (not 55) dc.

Row 16 (RS) With B, rep row 8.

Row 17 (WS) With A, rep row 9 only work 35 (not 51) dc. Cut A.

Row 18 (WS) With B, rep row 2.

Row 19 (WS) With A, rep row 3 only with 31 (not 63) dc.

Row 20 (RS) With B, rep row 4.

Row 21 (WS) With C, rep row 5 only with 27 (not 59) dc.

Row 22 (WS) With B, rep row 6.

Row 23 (RS) With A, rep row 7 only with 23 (not 55) dc.

Row 24 (RS) With B, rep row 8.

Row 25 (WS) With A, rep row 9 only with 19 (not 51) dc. Cut A.

Row 26 (WS) With B, rep row 2.

Row 27 (WS) With A, rep row 3 only with 15 (not 63) dc.

Row 28 (RS) With B, rep row 4.

Row 29 (WS) With C, rep row 5 only with 11 (not 59) dc.

Row 30 (WS) With B, rep row 6.

Row 31 (RS) With A, rep row 7 only with 7 (not 55) dc.

Row 32 (RS) With B, rep row 8.

Row 33 (WS) With A, rep row 9 only with 3 (not 51) dc.

Row 34 (WS) With B, rep row 2—14 sl sts.

Row 35 (RS) With A, working in both loops, ch 2, work 2 dc, 2 hdc, 2 sc, skip 2 sts, work 2 sc, 2 hdc, 2 dc. Cut yarn

102000000	Needle Art	4.99
102000000	Needle Art	3.99
105000000	Crafts	11.99
105000000	Crafts	1.99
102000000	Needle Art	9.99
105000000	Crafts	7.79

COUPON CODE: 43551
40 % Off Coupon (12.99-5.20)

SUBTOTAL	40.74
TAX TOTAL	3.36

TOTAL   44.10

VISA   44.10
ACCOUNT #: ************2089
AUTH#: 015157
ACCT: VISA   INSERTED
    US DEBIT
CARD # ************2089   EXP **/**
REF #   AUTH #   RESP 00
115101301042   015157   ISO 00
AID: A0000000980840
TSI: 6800 ARC:00 CUR:0840
TVR: 8080088000
APP: US DEBIT
IAD: 06010A0360A000

--Continued on Side 2--

Total sa...

Than...
   Beco...
Return Po... ...eceip...

Visit our website ...lobby.com

0402002066390...0215

1/30/21   11:50 AM

HOBBY LOBBY.

Super Savings, Super Selection!

RETURN POLICY

Hobby Lobby values customer satisfaction,
with or without the receipt.

WITH ORIGINAL SALES RECEIPT:

Within 90 days of purchase, we will gladly exchange the
merchandise, give a store credit, or issue a refund based on
the original method of payment. There will be a wait of 10
calendar days on check purchases, or merchandise credit can
be issued.*

WITHOUT ORIGINAL SALES RECEIPT:

You may exchange the merchandise or be issued a
merchandise credit based on the lowest selling price in the
last 60 days. Valid ID is required.

*Returns or exchanges of Sewing and Embroidery machines,
Silhouette® and Cricut® products are prohibited unless
customer presents original receipt and products are in new,
unopened condition. Warranty claims must be submitted
directly to the manufacturer.

We reserve the right to limit or refuse to accept the return of
certain products and non-receipted items.

    You Tube

and fold at center of the V, and seam the center tog.

FINISHING
Upper edge trim
Row 1 From the WS with A, ch 1 and work 114 sc along the upper edge, turn.
Row 2 (WS) Ch 2, 2 hdc in first st, hdc in each st to last st, 2 hdc in last st. Fasten off. Sew in ends. ◼

Jack Deutsch

Easy Striped Tote

Yarn (4)
Any worsted weight cotton yarn
- 10oz/285g or 475yd/435m in navy (A)
- 5oz/145g or 240yd/220m cream (B)

Hook
- Size F/5 (3.75mm) crochet hook *or size to obtain gauge*

Notions
- Stitch marker

LEARN BY VIDEO
www.go-crafty.com
- basic stripes
- ch (chain)
- crocheting in the round
- hdc (half double crochet)
- sc (single crochet)
- sc2tog (single crochet 2 sts tog)

MEASUREMENTS
- **Circumference (above base)** 30"/76cm
- **Length** 13"/33cm

GAUGE
14 sts and 13 rnds to 4"/10cm over stripe pattern using size F/5 (3.75mm) hook. *Take time to check gauge.*

STITCH GLOSSARY
Stripe Pattern
Rnd 1 With A, ch 2, pm in top of ch, hdc in each hdc around, join with sl st to marked ch, remove marker.
Rnd 2 With A, ch 1, pm in top of ch, sc in each hdc to last hdc, work sc but use new color for 2nd yo of sc, cont with new color, join with sl st to marked ch, remove marker.
Rnd 3 With B, rep rnd 1.
Rnd 4 With B, rep rnd 2.
Rep rnds 1–4 for stripe pat.

NOTE
Bag is worked in joined rnds. Do not turn work.

BODY
With A, ch 106. Hdc into 3rd ch from hook, hdc into each ch across—105 sts.
Do not turn work. Join with sl st into beg ch. Ch 1, place marker (pm) into this ch, sc into each hdc around. Cont in stripe pat, moving marker to top of ch for each rnd, until rnd 1 of the 3rd B stripe is complete.
Next (dec) rnd With B, ch 1, sc into next hdc, sc2tog, sc into each of next 50 hdc, sc2tog, work sc to end of rnd—103 sts.
Cont in stripe pat until rnd 1 of the 5th B stripe is complete.
Next (dec) rnd With B, ch 1, sc into next hdc, sc2tog, sc into each of next 49 hdc, sc2tog, work sc to end of rnd—101 sts.
Cont in stripe pat until rnd 1 of the 7th A stripe is complete.
Next (dec) rnd With A, ch 1, sc into next hdc, sc2tog, sc into each of next 48 hdc, sc2tog, work sc to end of rnd—99 sts.

Cont in stripe pattern until 16 stripes are complete, being sure to change to A at end of last rnd.

Top
Rnd 1 Ch 2, pm in top of ch, hdc in each st around, join with sl st in marked st, remove marker.
Rep rnd 1 twice more.
Rnd 4 (strap openings) Ch 2, 5 hdc into next 5 hdc, ch 4, skip next 4 hdc, *hdc into next 10 hdc, ch 5, skip next 5 hdc, hdc into next 10 hdc, ch 4, skip next 4 hdc*; rep from * to *, end hdc in next 6 hdc, join with sl st to beg ch.
Next rnd Ch 2, 5 hdc in next 5 hdc, 4 hdc into ch-sp, *hdc in next 10 hdc, 5 hdc into ch-sp, hdc in next 10 hdc, 4 hdc into ch-sp*; rep from * to *, end hdc in next 6 hdc, join with sl st to beg ch.
Rep rnd 1 twice. Fasten off.

BASE
Ch 44.
Inc rnd 1 Hdc into 3rd ch from hook, hdc into next 41 ch sts, hdc 3 times into next ch—46 sts. Place marker in center st of hdc 3. Do not turn. Working into other side of ch, hdc to last st, hdc 3 times in last st, place marker in center stitch of hdc 3, join with sl st to beg of rnd—92 hdc in rnd.
Inc rnd 2 Ch 2, hdc into same st as ch-2, hdc to 1 st before marked st, hdc 2 times into next hdc, remove marker, hdc 3 times into marked st, mark center stitch, hdc 2 times into next st, hdc into each hdc to 1 st before next marker, hdc 2 times into next st, remove marker, hdc 3 times into next st, place marker in center st of hdc 3, join with sl st to beg ch—8 sts inc'd.
Rep inc rnd 2 three times more—124 sts. Fasten off.

Easy Striped Tote

FINISHING

Sew base into lower edge of bag.

Straps

Ch 90. Work 1 hdc into 3rd ch from
hook, work 1 hdc into each ch—89 sts.
Turn.
Next row Ch 2, hdc in each hdc across.
Do not turn. Working into other side of
ch, work 1 hdc into each ch. Fasten off.
Insert end of strap through one opening
at top of bag. Loop strap around top of
bag and sew end to strap. Rep for other
end.
Rep for 2nd strap.

Ties

Make a chain 40"/101.5cm long. Fasten off. Pull tie ends from front to back
through strap holes, bring ends tog
from back to front through center hole.
Make knot around strand at front (see
photo). Rep for other side. ■